The D

by Jenny (
Photography by Ly

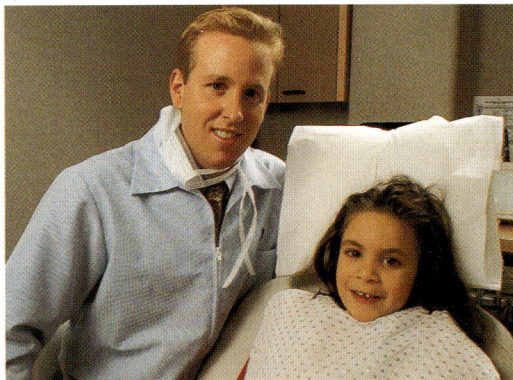

NELSON PRICE MILBURN

I am going to see the dentist.
The dentist is going
to look at my teeth.

Mum will stay here
in the waiting room.

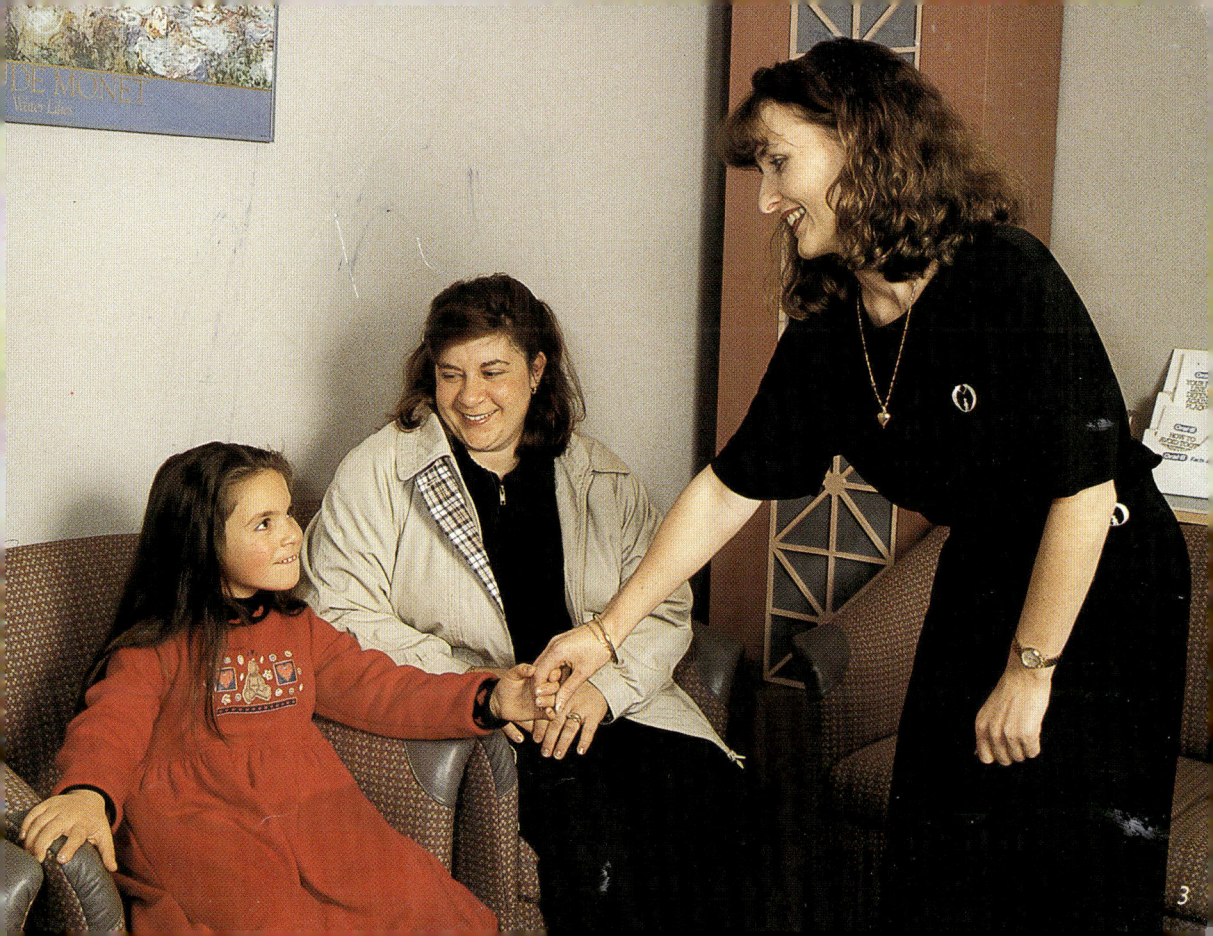

The nurse helps me
to get up onto the big chair.
I can see some pink mouthwash.

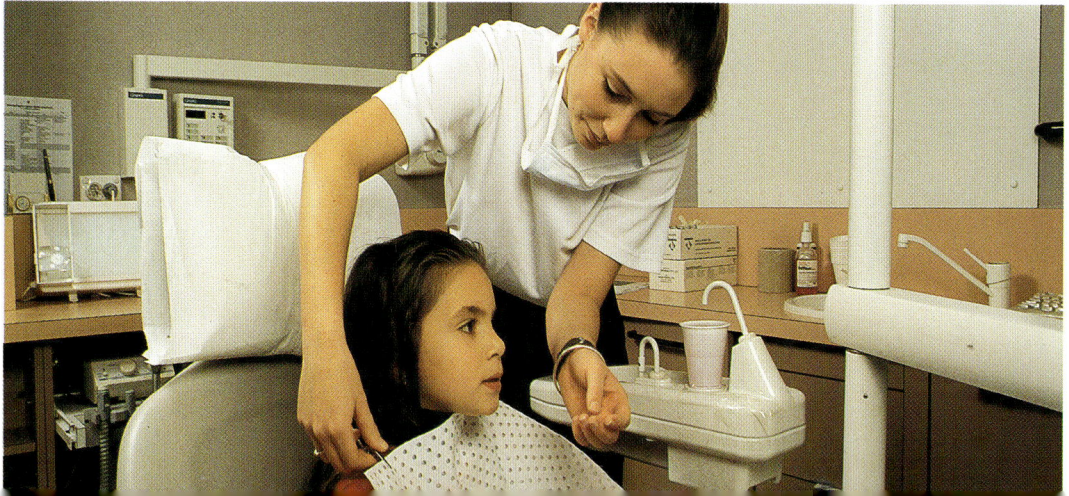

I can see a tray
with some instruments on it.

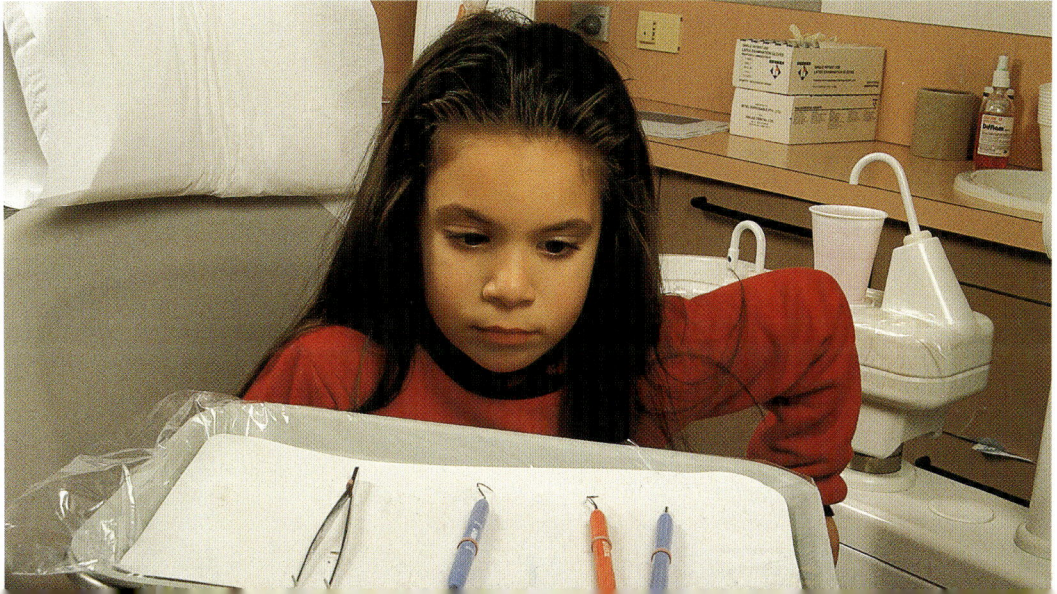

The dentist puts on his mask and his gloves.

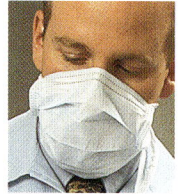

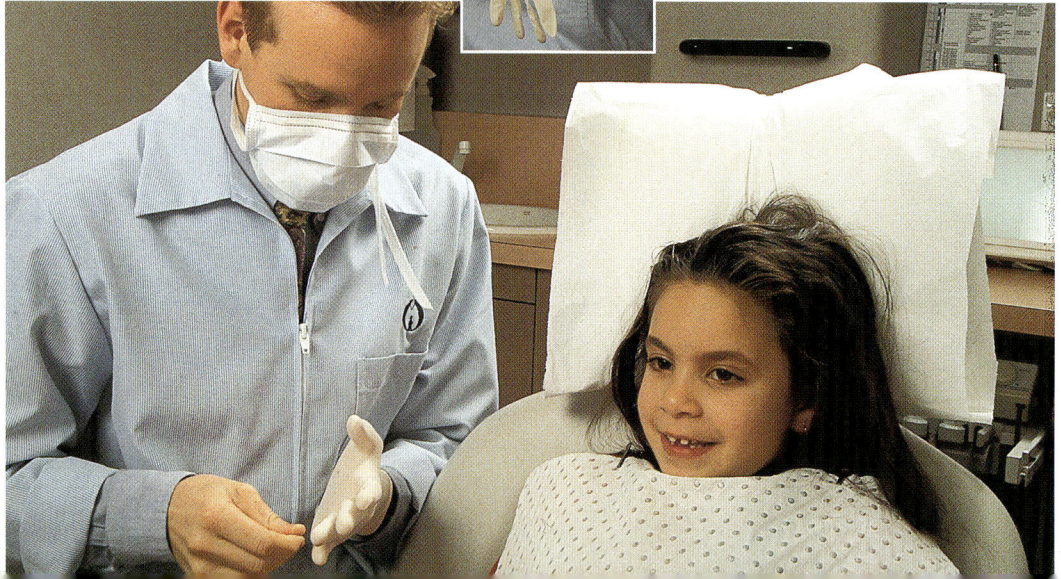

Then he makes the chair go back.

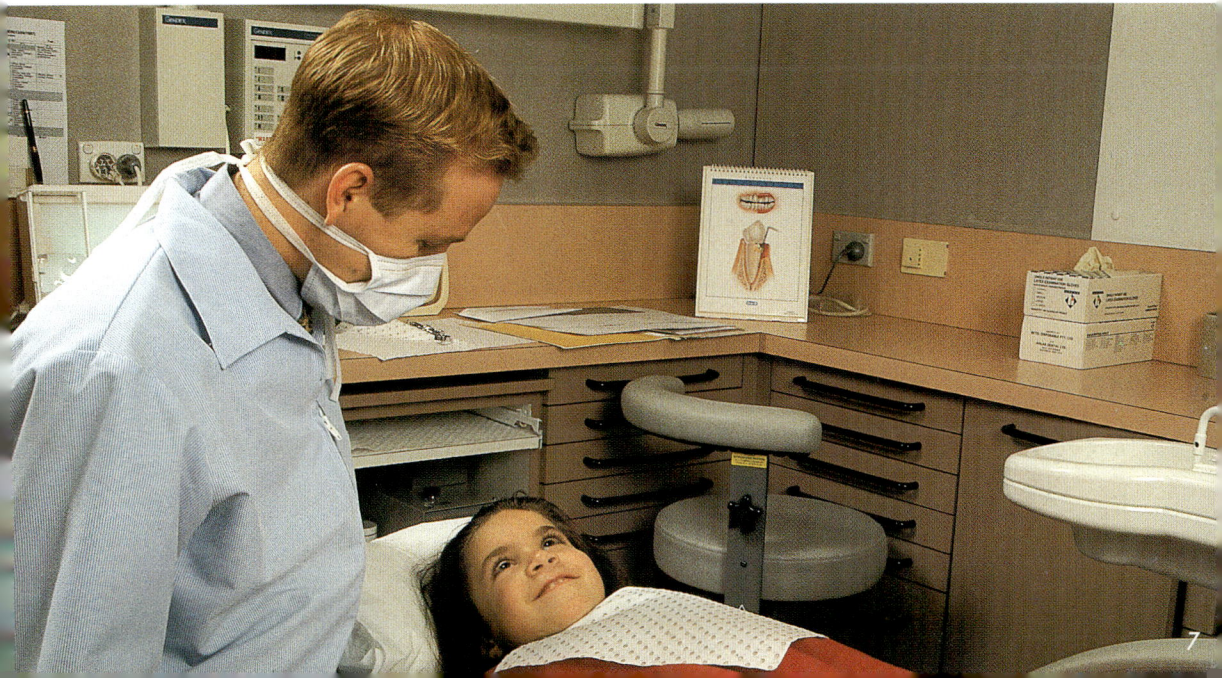

I look up at the light.
The dentist puts some glasses
on me, so that the light
will not hurt my eyes.

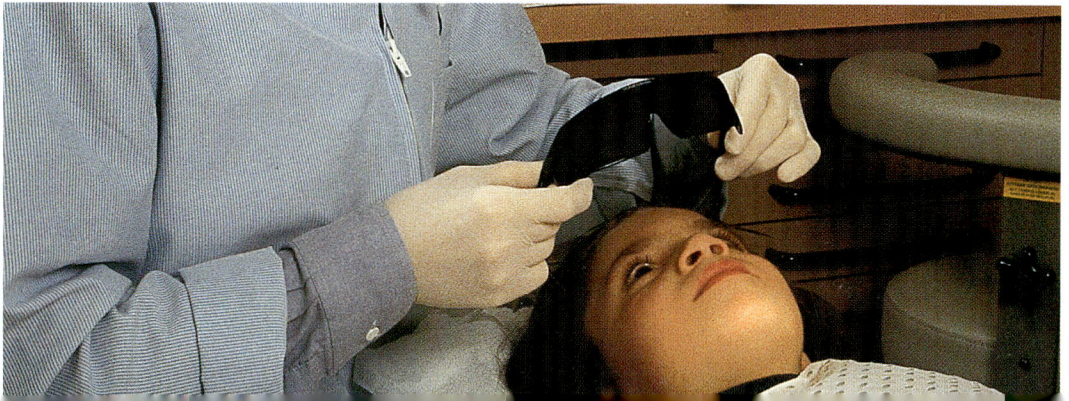

The dentist looks inside my mouth.

He looks at all my teeth.

He finds a hole

in one of my back teeth.

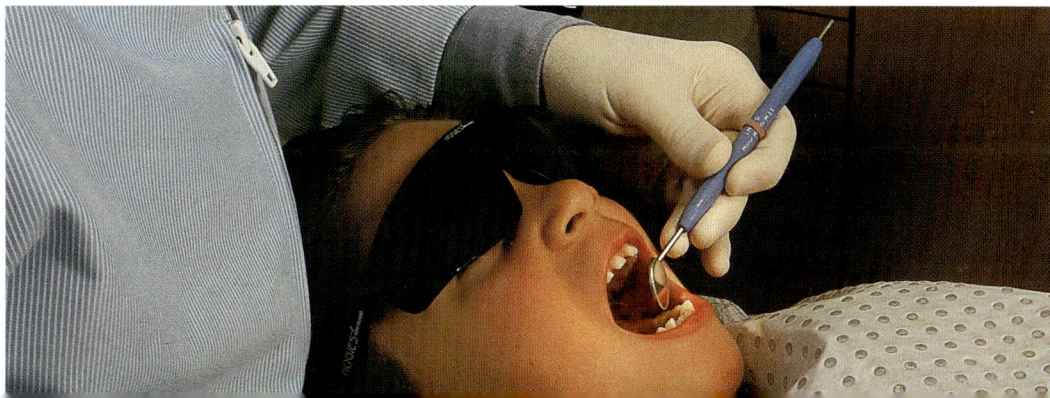

I have to stay very still.
The dentist makes my tooth
go numb, so that it will not hurt.

My mouth goes numb, too.

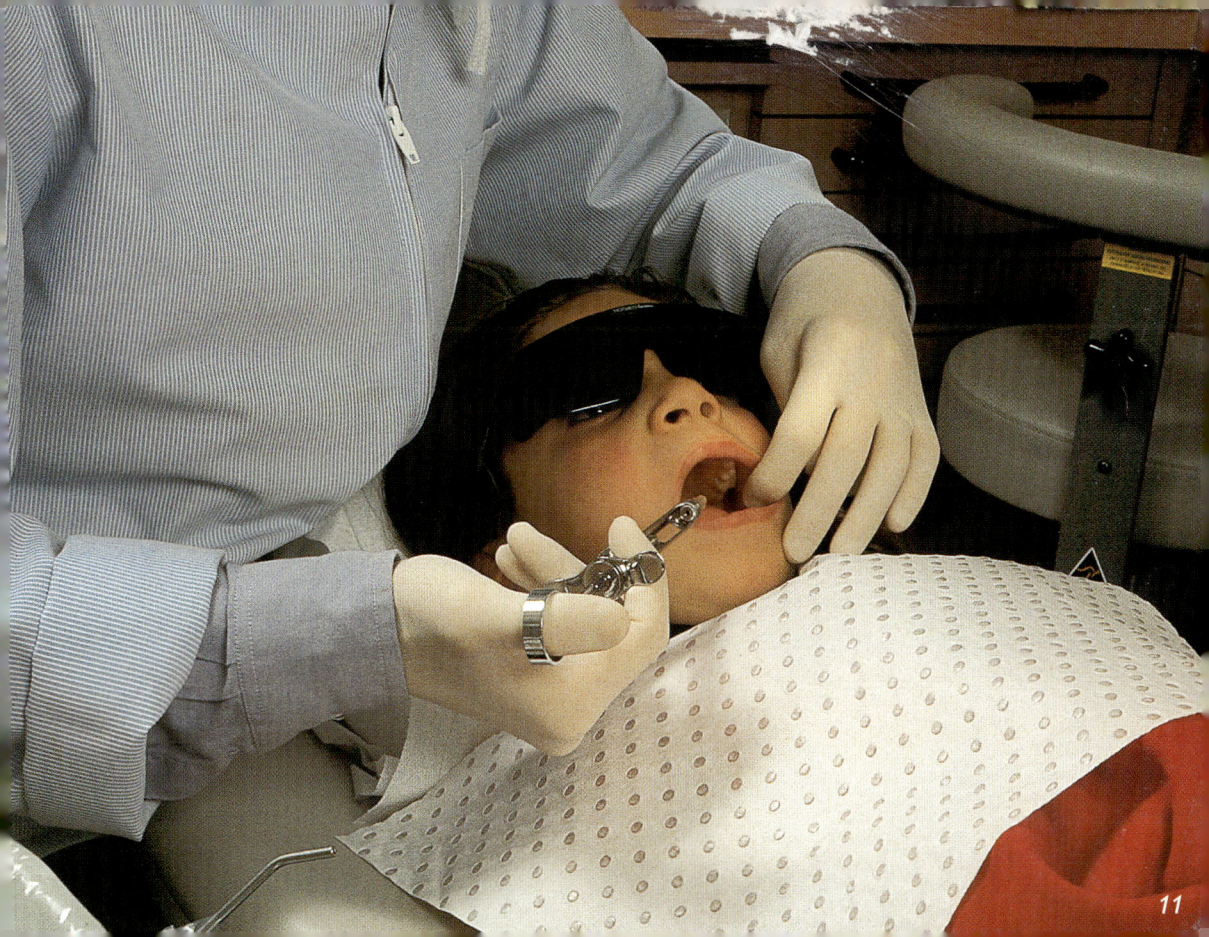

The dentist cleans out the hole in my tooth with the drill. Then he fills the hole.

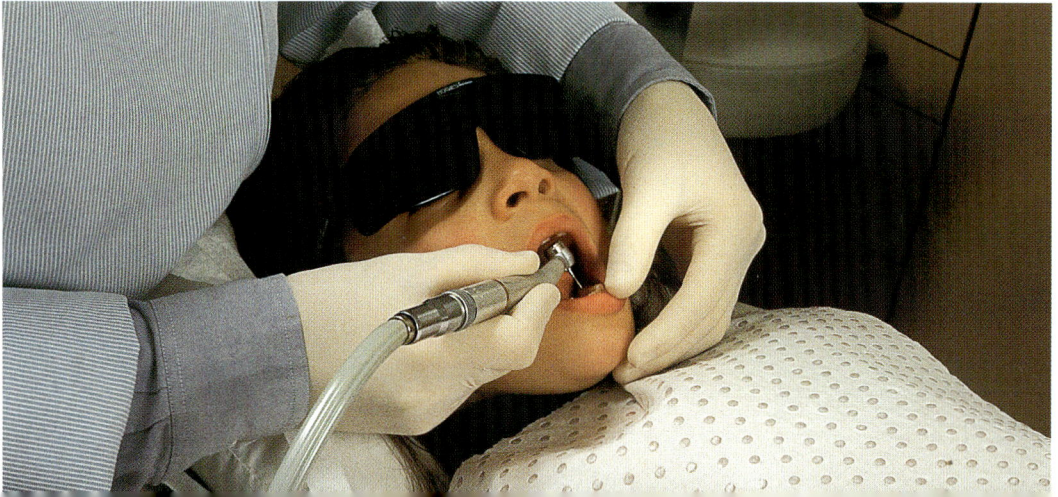

Now I can wash out my mouth with the pink mouthwash.

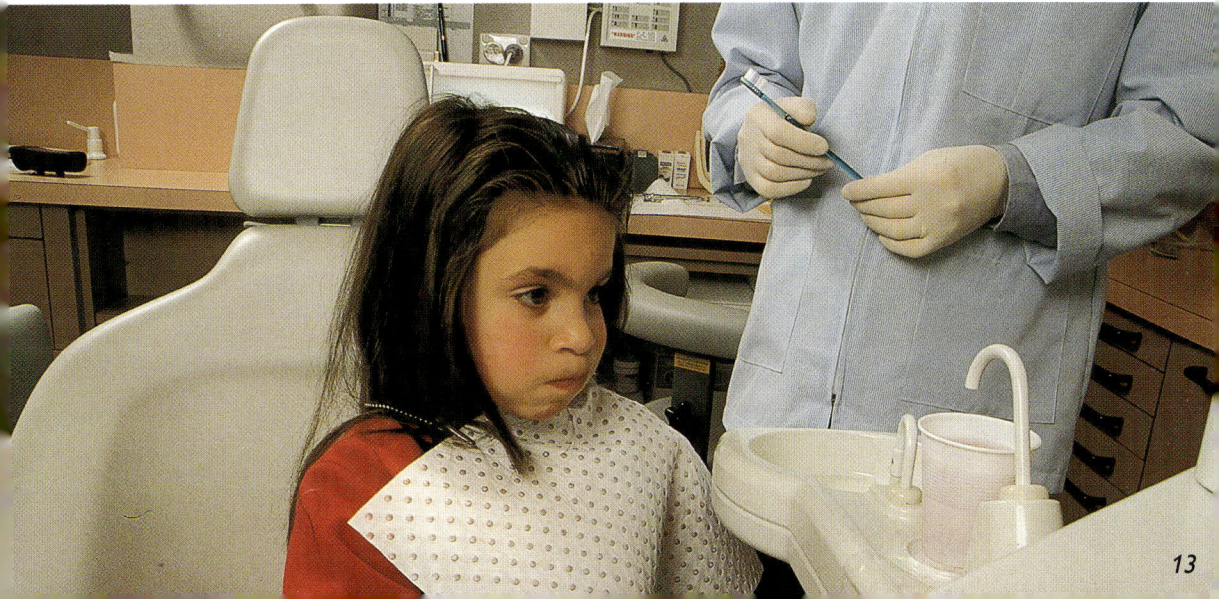

Then the dentist shows me the way to brush my teeth.
The big teeth look funny.

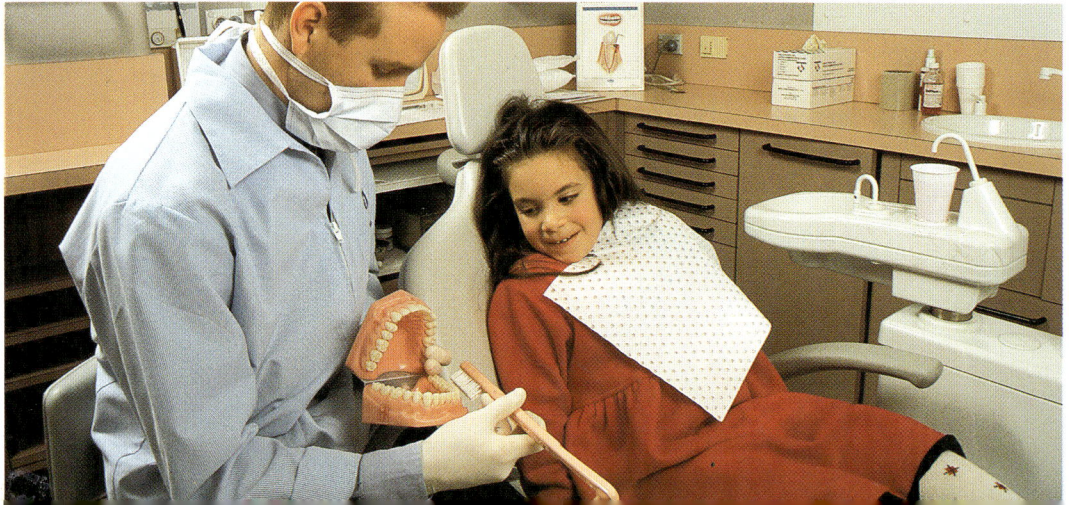

The dentist helps me
to brush my teeth, too.

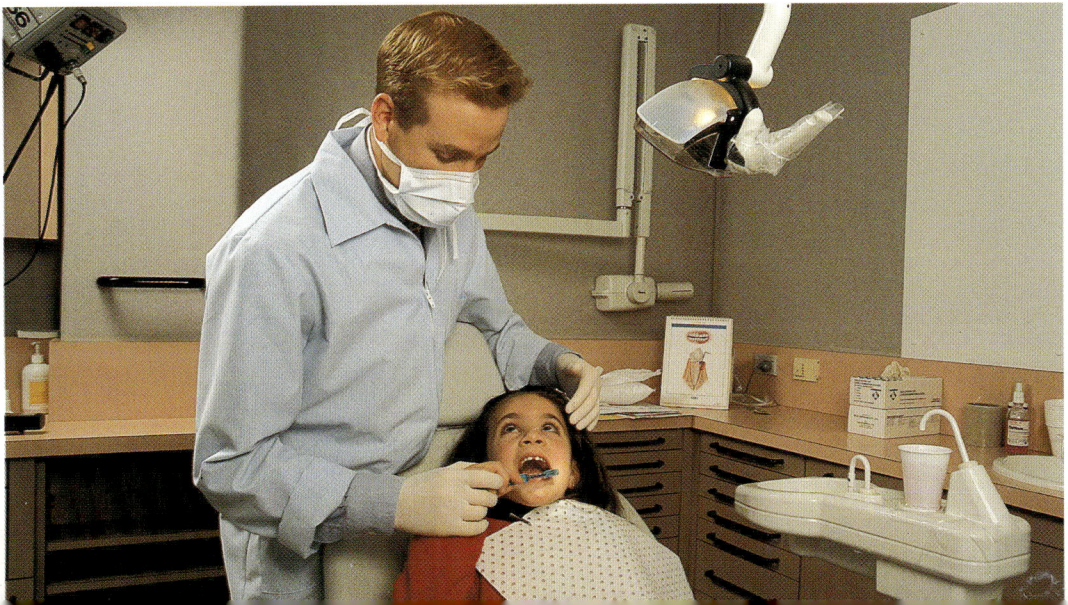

I run to Mum and I show her
where the dentist filled my tooth.

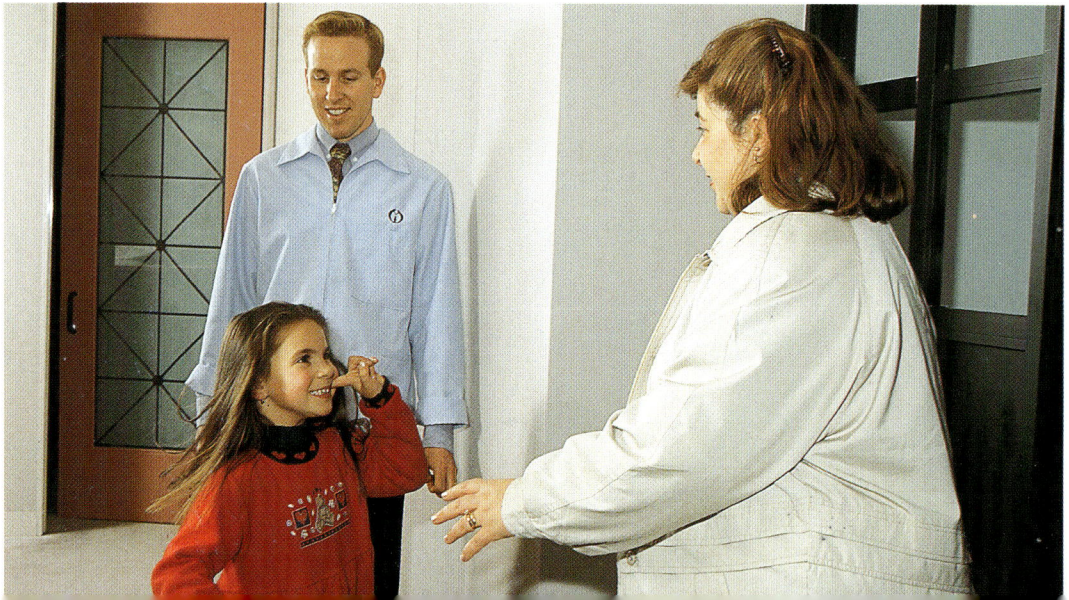